LEADERSHIP
ACCOUNTABILITY IN
GOVERNMENT

LEADERSHIP
ACCOUNTABILITY IN
GOVERNMENT

Defining, Measuring &
Managing for Results

Richard Demeritte

Library of Congress Control Number:		2016908878
ISBN:	Hardcover	978-1-5245-0595-0
	Softcover	978-1-5245-0594-3
	eBook	978-1-5245-0593-6

Print information available on the last page

Rev. date: 06/06/2016

To order additional copies of this book, contact:
Xlibris
1-888-795-4274
www.Xlibris.com
Orders@Xlibris.com
726214

CONTENTS

Acknowledgments

THE RT. HON. DAME JOAN SAWYER
PATRON, CHARTERED INSTITUTE OF
ARBITRATORS (CIArb) BAHAMAS
FORMER CHIEF JUSTICE OF THE BAHAMAS
FORMER PRESIDENT COURT OF APPEAL

As far as I am aware, this is a second book authored by His Excellency Richard C. Demeritte, Esq., retired ambassador for his country and a former Auditor General of The Bahamas.

While it is another book about leadership, the author concentrates on the qualities of outstandingly good leaders: self-disciplined, honest, sober minded, gentle, hospitable, and willing to be open and accountable for their conduct while holding public office.

This is particularly significant at this point in The Bahamas as well as world history because of the present turmoil facing so many ostensibly civilized and democratic nations.

It is to be hoped that those who are presently in leadership positions as well as those who aspire to such positions will "read, learn, mark, and inwardly digest" the contents of this book and then put its principles into action to the benefit of their fellow citizens.

Joan A. Sawyer, DBE

December 30, 2015

Acknowledgment
Leadership Accountability in Government

The words *leadership* and *accountability* are two words the world thirsts for on a daily basis. Civil societies around the world continue their demand for leaders who are accountable.

Good leaders are accountable, and this accountability leads to transparency, which allows everyone to feel a part of the system. Accountability means that you are responsible for your actions.

I first met Dr. Richard Demeritte at the Department of the Auditor General where I worked under Dr. Demeritte's leadership during his tenure as the Auditor General of the Commonwealth of The Bahamas. This is where I saw him demonstrate the principles of leadership and accountability. He was always a professional extraordinaire and demanded one's best. These principles have assisted me in becoming the leader that I am today.

It has always been Dr. Demeritte's heart's desire to encourage and mentor future leaders; this book will undoubtedly successfully achieve its goal.

I am convinced that the manuscript Leadership Accountability in Government is unique, transformative, and will set the course for leadership and accountability not only nationally but also internationally. I am greatly enriched by the dynamic principles contained in this book.

It is my belief that current and future leaders will use Dr. Richard Demeritte's book as an indispensable resource nationally and internationally.

Terrance Bastian
Auditor General of the Commonwealth of The Bahamas

Ambassador Sean McWeeney, QC
Former Attorney General, Commonwealth of The Bahamas
Former Senator, Government of The Bahamas

December 2015

I am honored to have been invited to provide the acknowledgment for this new and important book by Dr. Richard Demeritte. I hope it wins a wide readership both at home and abroad. It imparts refreshing and valuable insights into leadership and accountability—insights that are deserving of close study not only in The Bahamas but also around the world. Indeed, I would commend this book not only to politicians and other public servants but to all those who aspire to positions of leadership, whether it be in churches, in businesses, in their professions, in civic or community upliftment organizations, or even in the family.

Drawing on a wide range of historical examples and the wealth of his own experience in government, international diplomacy, the accountancy profession, business, and the church, Dr. Demeritte combines his impressive intellect with his capacity for clear and concise expression to write a book that is both provocative and compelling. He explores some of the finer points of leadership and the phenomenon of power while forthrightly addressing the responsibilities that these entail.

Leaders can be taught and trained to achieve, and then maintain, the correct balance between the exercise of power and the observance of the basic tenets of accountability. That is Dr. Demeritte's central message, and he articulates it in a way that is both profound and persuasive.

It is my sincere hope that this book will serve as both a lamp of inspiration and a navigational aid for all those who are either preparing for, or are already exercising, leadership in one sphere of human endeavor or another. There is an abundance of practical wisdom to be found within the pages that follow.

I extend warmest congratulations to Dr. Demeritte on this latest literary accomplishment of his and wish him continued success in all his endeavors.

H.E. Sean McWeeney, QC
Nassau, Bahamas

December 30, 2015

Book Endorsement for Richard C. Demeritte

I am delighted to endorse and celebrate the literary work of a consummate Bahamian diplomat.

Dr. Richard C. Demeritte's manifesto on *Leadership Accountability in Governance* is timely and compelling.

Social and political revolutions, historically, have a common origin. People revolt because of the lack of authentic leadership, transparency, and accountability in governance.

Inherent in our human nature is the need to lead and be led by those we deem worthy. As leaders, we voluntarily give honor to our political authorities with the hope that they respect the wishes of the electorate through transparency, accountability, and natural justice.

In Dr. Demerrite's work, he utilizes his vast experiences as a statesman and a diplomat, as well as the discipline of his vocation, to crystallize how leadership ought to benefit the people and why accountability is critical to success and good governance.

He is a man graced with credibility. This is because he has consistently lived a life of accountability, transparency, and high ethical standards. Just as these traits shaped his character and foundation the contents of this latest achievement I trust it will shape the ethos of the young people and adults alike.

As Speaker of the Honorable House of Assembly, I am encouraged by the information that will be disseminated to students in our school system. It should be a constantly available source and resource for a greater understanding of civil society, leadership, and government.

Leadership is inherent in each us, and our duty is to discover and refine our gifts and serve them to the world. Governments are essentially a group of leaders chosen by leaders to serve their interest in national governance. The greatest challenge nations face in the execution of this ideal is identifying authentic leaders who use their gifts, power, and influence for the greater good of mankind.

William Pitt, former British Prime Minister, said in a speech to the UK House of Lords in 1770: "Unlimited power is apt to corrupt the minds of those who possess it."

Since this truth was uttered in 1770 and democracies have grappled with the principles of separation of powers and the application of appropriate checks and balances, nations seek to codify the powers of the executive in an effort to create a more measured and just society.

The Commonwealth of The Bahamas has enshrined this requirement in article 72(1) in its constitution as one but several measures to promote freedom and rights to the people.

It is my prayer that this manifesto engenders further conversations and debates that deepen our democracy and advance the cause of social development of our people.

Hon. Dr. Kendal V. O. Major, MP, JP
Speaker House of Assembly

Acknowledgment

Leadership Accountability in Government

When I got the call last Friday from my dear friend and colleague H. E. Dr. Richard Demeritte, asking me to write an acknowledgment to his book-in-the-making *Leadership Accountability in Government*, my first reaction was, wow, what a great honor is this for me for this giant of a man whom I have known for over twenty years to ask of me such a request.

He then sent me scripts of the book at 2:00 a.m. That's when his mind's brilliance coupled with his body's energy is working at full capacity.

Accountability in public office is nothing but a reflection of His Excellency's life experience—a life full of integrity, respect, honor, service, humility, sacrifices, but powered with leadership and the love of country.

Leadership Accountability in Government is an amazing book that combines leadership and the process of accountability that is described step by step, which I, as an engineer, found interesting and intriguing.

This book can be easily used as a manual for persons seeking political office, for those studying political science, and for all high school students who are seeking to learn discipline and leadership.

In closing, I can say that I am not surprised that my dear friend HE Richard Demeritte came up with this title for the book, which I believe will serve this country's populace and the world in general in all facets of life to prepare individuals for honest and clean representation in their respective societies.

Tony Joudi
Ambassador

FOREWORD

By the Rt. Hon. Perry G. Christie
Prime Minister and Minister of Finance

It is a momentous event when one fulfills an ambition to write and then publish a book of this kind. It signals the culmination of a great deal of introspection and research harnessed to a burning desire by the author to memorialize his words in a way that will endure for many years, even generations, to come.

That is certainly the paradigm of this latest work by Dr. Richard Demeritte, and he should be very proud of the end product.

It is particularly pleasing that Dr. Demeritte has taken the time to give us his precious and timely insights into *Leadership Accountability in Government*, the title of this new book. He takes as his central theme the need for those of us who hold positions of public trust to be ever cognizable of our overarching duty to be answerable to the public we are dedicated to serving. Dr. Demeritte develops this theme in a way that has urgent relevance not only to serving public servants but to all aspirants to public office as well.

There are three main parts to this book: leadership overview, accountability in government, and structural framework for accountability and transparency.

On the first of these three themes—leadership—Dr. Demeritte emphasizes that we are all, in one way or another, leaders, provided, of course, that we exhibit the ability to bring people together and cause them to join in the common pursuit of an objective or point of view.

It is Dr. Demeritte's contention that such leadership is most notable when it emerges from a moral conviction as to the rightness of a particular cause. Leadership is not confined to the political arena, however, but is found in all spheres of human endeavor. In this regard, Dr. Demeritte draws on three well-known historical figures, each an outstanding leader in his own right: Julius Caesar, Winston Churchill, and the Rev. Dr. Martin Luther King. Although worlds apart in their leadership styles and backgrounds, all three demonstrated strength of leadership and all three were prepared to suffer massive personal disappointments and major career setbacks. In the end, however, they were vindicated, and the fruits of their leadership are still of enormous benefit to mankind.

Similarly, in his chapters on accountability framework in government" and accountability in government, Dr. Demeritte gives specific examples of accountability. He goes to some length to introduce the reader, especially the neophyte or novice public servant, to various forms of accountability both from the technical/legislative perspective and from the individual or "personal value system" perspective as well.

The most compelling part of the book, in my view, is Dr. Demeritte's emphasis on accountability to the populace and the need for transparency: the public have a right to know about the actions of the government that is sworn to serve them. This makes for interesting and provocative reading, and the lessons the author imparts are worthy of the closest study.

I wish to commend and congratulate Dr. Demeritte on this important new book of his. He is, by profession, an accountant. He has served the Bahamian people in a variety of roles, most notably as Auditor General of The Bahamas and then later as our High Commissioner (Ambassador) to the Court of King James in the UK. He fully understands the key precepts and structures of governance not just in the academic sense but in the context of the "real world" service that he has rendered over the years with great distinction and patriotic devotion.

It is my fervent hope that this book will meet with a wide reception and that its timeless lessons of accountability will both inform and inspire present and future generations of public servants both in The Bahamas and abroad.

Perry G. Christie
Prime Minister and Minister of Finance
Commonwealth of The Bahamas

THIS BOOK IS DEDICATED

To my lovely wife, Ruth, for her kindness, devotion,
and in celebration of our golden anniversary.

Richard C. Demeritte, PhD

Special Tribute to Dr. Myles Munroe, OBE

It is a good thing to pay tribute to leaders who fear the Lord. I am delighted to honor the accomplishments of my friend, the late Dr. Myles E. Munroe, OBE, founding president and senior pastor of Bahamas Faith Ministries International, Myles Munroe International, and the International Third World Leaders Association.

We celebrate a fearless man and the career of a courageous and dedicated visionary. My beloved friend Myles was a man who strived to see what might be and to turn challenges into visible and tangible solutions.

Dr. Myles Munroe was truly a multitalented leader in his field, and it was simply impossible not to admire, like, and respect him. He created a new standard of moral conduct and brought tremendous insight to accountability deliberations in his usual vigor, passion, and profound insight. His breadth of knowledge and skilful participation across a wide spectrum of biblical issues has greatly assisted the work and effectiveness of churches and governments worldwide. And his strength of character was embodied in his ability to create a dynamic and cooperative working environment within various circles of churches and governments.

His unique leadership style facilitated Christian development and an appreciation for one another's points of view. In the best tradition, Dr. Munroe steered the kingdomship of state for many years and helped develop and nurture the shared vision of the kingdom.

There have been many powerful people in the history of our world long remembered for their dedication to positively influence mankind. Their journey to success started with the belief that they were capable of doing it by living from their hearts.

As individuals, we have the power within to become something bigger than the life we live. No matter where we came from, or what we are doing with our life now, there is always room for sharing those simple and amazing qualities that make us unique.

The weight of our daily lives sometimes deters us from taking the first step to change our ways to grow within ourselves and visualize our true potential. However, when mind over matter becomes a part of our whole being as demonstrated by Dr. Myles Munroe, anything is possible. But we must be able to see the invisible in order to do the impossible, and the choices we make will reveal the true nature of our character.

My first encounter with Dr. Myles was in 1985 when we met in London, and in our conversation, he said clearly and emphatically that his purpose in life was to change the world. I believe he was well on his way to accomplish his life objective. This makes us wonder about the difference between ordinary and extraordinary leaders.

Only those who dare to courageously take risks and initiative can reach extraordinary heights. It follows that leaders are constantly being developed on a daily basis and not within a day. Personal growth does not happen in a single moment but over a long slow process. If you aspire to accomplish something great, then be prepared to devote a great amount of time to it. To be extraordinary leaders, we can neither run from reality nor shut our eyes to it. We have to see our present situation as it actually is and not only as we wish it would be.

Ordinary people change their circumstances to improve their lives instead of changing themselves to improve their circumstances. They change just enough to get away from their problems but not enough to solve them. Extraordinary people, on the other hand, realize that in order to achieve better results, they must continually improve themselves by upgrading their abilities and leadership skills.

A real leader creates focus and strives to paint an inspiring vision. As individuals, we want to be a part of something greater than ourselves. A real leader should paint this inspiring vision and then articulate the priorities to help people know how to make progress against that vision.

All leaders cast a shadow; the question is whether yours is blocking the sun or inspiring others with its silhouette to strive for more. Leaders need to model the behavior they want their organizations to emulate, which was the life of my friend, colleague and brother in Christ, my spiritual leader and close confidant: the late Dr. Myles Munroe.

INTRODUCTION

Foundation of Accountability

Parliament and the Treasury: The Problem of Accountability

The Treasury emerged from the reign of Charles II with its institutional character greatly enhanced. The Treasury and its rulers were drawn more deeply than ever into the parliamentary world, forced to evolve techniques of collaboration with an intractable and inquisitorial House of Commons. The autonomy of the Treasury could not yet be taken for granted.

"Accountability," in this context of Treasury history, is a problem one might risk defining simply as the task of enforcing the prompt accurate discharge of responsibility by those handling public money. Unfortunately, however, the task was in no way simple or one the Treasury could perform alone.

It also required an independent agency (the reformed Exchequer) empowered to issue these appropriated funds to a responsible nonpolitical paymasters, disbursing funds on behalf of government departments. Finally, it required an effective machinery for the independent audit of this expenditure (Auditor General) and of the submission of the balanced annual account to the scrutinizing committee of the House of Commons (PAC). This brought the process of public expenditure full circle, laying before parliament the means of checking that its estimates and appropriations had been adhered to.

The problem of accountability could be regarded from the Treasury's point of view as the deceptively simple one of making the Exchequer do its job. It was the Exchequer, and in particular the Upper Exchequer or Exchequer of Accounts, that carried the primary responsibility for the audit of accounts and the prosecution of defaulters, things that it could be expected to do without prorating and only the minimum of Treasury intervention.

The essence of Exchequer audit, throughout the centuries, had been a judicious process by which accountants were formally examined about their registered abilities and, if they could produce evidence that they had discharged them, were legally acquitted of further responsibility.

Tardy and archaic, the processes of Exchequer audit were not designed to produce an accurate or comprehensive account of what was really happening to public funds. The obstacles were partly conceptual ones, a failure to perceive precisely what the problem required.

In larger part, they were institutional obstacles, conservative resistance officials with a vested interest in anachronism. Needless to say, they presented their case in high-minded terms as guardians of a sacred and immemorial trust, but the material, and very comfortable, foundation of their position was stated simply in their security of tenure.

Nearly all the major officials of the Exchequer (including the chancellor) held their places for life. Some officers, such as the lord treasurers and the clerk of the Pells, were virtually hereditary. They were immune to displacement for inefficiency and remarkably resistant to charges of dishonesty, performing their duties only through deputies, and they pocketed their fees and defied the administrative sanctions of the Treasury. It should come as no surprise to learn that the Treasury Commissioners of 1667 were not prepared to acquiesce in this situation.

The Treasury Establishment: The Problem of Professionalism

The earliest budget was presented in 1890 when Gladstone recognized the incapability of the Treasury's officials to provide him with any technical assistance.

Long before the midnineteenth century, the Treasury had been obliged to recognize, if not fully comprehend, the administrative shortcomings of its permanent staff and the piecemeal responses of the department.

There were even intervals when the requirements of the Treasury seemed modest enough to be matched by the abilities, and exceeded by the numbers, of its permanent staff. Consequently, the line of development is a rather patchy one, sometimes difficult to document, and underlying its hesitance in the same kind of shortcoming, which hampered the development of effective accountability, the Treasury's failure to identify precisely what the problem was.

In 1823, a relatively junior Treasury clerk addressed himself to a careful analysis of the Treasury's organizational problems, reaching an exhaustive, logical solution. He was able to do this largely because he, rather than the lords of the Treasury, was best placed to appreciate what the problems required and what they had so signally failed to get.

His careful diagnosis, rooted in a sound understanding of the establishment's recent history, is the unique exception among Treasury memoranda, which proves the general rule that the transient political heads of the Treasury were generally incapable of discerning what measures were most likely to induce their efforts to give of their best. It was to be some years before the Treasury board's solemn injunctions to arrive punctually, work harder, and merit promotion gave way to enlightened efforts at the management of Treasury careers.

His evolution as a major figure in English administration was far more pronounced, although like the clerks, he enjoyed only a precarious official tenure.

The Secretary, however, was the beneficiary of the process by which, in 1673, the parliamentary management was passed from the hands of the Secretaries of State to those of the Treasury. The confidential power and public prestige of the Secretary could scarcely grow higher. With Henry Guy's successor, however, the administrative dimension of the secretaryship was firmly reinstated. William Lowndes was the nearest thing to a professional civil servant the post had yet produced, and despite his long and influential membership of the House of Commons, his role at the Treasury seems to anticipate that of a Permanent rather than a Parliamentary Secretary.

The Treasury, 1660-1872

The precedent set by Lowndes was followed when John Taylor, a Treasury clerk since 1692, became Parliamentary Secretary. The early other examples are of Charles Lowndes, Joint Secretary after forty-one years' service as a Treasury official, and Edward Chamberlayne, who committed suicide in 1752 after twenty years in the Treasury. Thomas Bradshaw, the former war office clerk who became Joint Secretary after five years in the Treasury, is not such a significant example, but there are enough instances to show that the Lowndes precedent was successful.

Evidence suggests that by the end of the seventeenth century, the Treasury establishment was an embryo hierarchy of capable public servants, advancing by merit as well as seniority toward responsible and rewarding duties. From this context, therefore, there was nothing incongruous about William Lowndes becoming a leading public figure as Secretary to the Treasury.

The growing empire of revenue boards dependent upon the Treasury made its own contribution to the efforts, which helped pay for the War of the Spanish Succession, but as the Treasury's spokesman in the House of Commons and its representative on the Committee of Ways and Means, it was Lowndes as Secretary who consolidated the Treasury's mastery of parliamentary finance.

Relationship with Public Expenditure Committee

The order of reference of the Public Expenditure Committee requires it to have regard to matters raised in the annual reports of the Comptroller and Auditor General to parliament. It has therefore become customary for the Comptroller and Auditor General to discuss with the committee particular matters suggested for its consideration. The committee then prepares its own program of investigations comprising any of these matters and others that have come to its notice. When requested, senior representatives of the Audit Office attend on the committee for the purpose of relevant information. One senior officer attends all meetings of the committee for liaison purposes, and another member of the Audit Office staff is provided on secondment for research services to the committee.

These supplementary means of communication enable more specific information to be given, with greater detail, than in published reports. They also provide the opportunity to raise matters that may not have been referred to in the reports tabled in the House. The Audit Office cooperates with the committee, as far as it is proper to do so, in order that the scrutiny of financial management by parliament through the committee may be as effective as possible.

Comptroller and Auditor General in Westminster Parliamentary System

A basic principle of the Westminster system is that ultimate control over the raising of public revenue and its application should be exercised by parliament. The Comptroller and Auditor General is appointed to provide independent assurance to parliament that its will in these matters is carried out.

The comptroller and Auditor General is appointed by the Governor General on behalf of the Queen and is therefore an officer of the Crown, not an officer of parliament or a public servant.

For this reason, it is questionable whether parliament could direct the comptroller and Auditor General as to the scope or nature of his responsibilities, except by means of statutory appointment. Were it to be otherwise, the results would be a dangerous confusion between the function of an independent auditor and a servant of the House. It would be impossible to maintain the integrity of the audit function because the very independence upon which that integrity rests would be undermined.

This, of course, is to state the constitutional principle. In practice, as is known, no government in recent history in the Commonwealth has ever taken any steps that would infringe upon the independence of the Comptroller and Auditor General. It is relevant to state that the prohibition contained in the constitution against ministerial direction of the Auditor General (other than as administrative head of the department) is also a safeguard of his constitutional independent audit function.

The Comptroller and Auditor General role is principally carried out in the audit function, which encompasses the examination of the financial operations of the accounts of the government agencies. Basically, this function involves review of the control exercised over government revenue on whether the financial transactions or in the public accounts and other financial statements, that in exercising these responsibilities to ensures that the legislative will of parliament is carried out.

BRINGING ACCOUNTABILITY INTO FOCUS

Bringing accountability into focus is the most important Issue of our day, and we must define leadership to understand accountability. True accountability isn't consequences of our actions. Accountability is ownership.

Why leaders do not demand more accountability is one of the great mysteries of our times. Accountability is the concept in ethics and governance with several meanings. In leadership roles related to governance, accountability has been difficult to define.

Political accountability, however, is the accountability of the government, civil servants and politicians to the public, and to legislative bodies such as a congress or a parliament.

Ethical accountability also plays a progressively important role in academic fields, such as laboratory experiments and field research.

Accountability should therefore be defined as the "ultimate responsibility."

CHAPTER 1

Leadership Overview

Everyone has the innate ability to lead. Leadership exists in every sphere of life. People lead socially, professionally, spiritually, and at home in their family life. They become leaders because of their ability to guide others in pursuit of a common cause through their credibility that makes people want to follow them. It is their character and integrity that inspire others to follow them in fulfilling a guiding vision. They know the way forward and are able to inspire others to follow their lead.

Leaders exhibit many positive attributes such as self-confidence. They enjoy serving and commanding others and are capable of making their own decisions. True leaders exhibit leadership that is above reproach; they have a good reputation, are sober minded, live a well-balanced life, exercise self-discipline, and are able to teach others. Their leadership is gentle and hospitable; they stand ready to serve and are not covetous or lustful after money. True leaders are humble, courageous, and have a sense of humor. They demonstrate the qualities of patience, tact and diplomacy, inspirational power, and the executive ability to take action. They also pay a price for having to deal with criticisms, fatigue, loneliness, rejection, self-sacrifice, and the demands that come with having a family life.

We should aspire to develop our full leadership potential so we can be responsible leaders, goal-oriented leaders, growing leaders, decisive leaders, inspiring leaders, competent leaders, efficient leaders, unifying leaders, caring leaders, and working leaders desiring to follow the ultimate leader.

EFFECTIVE LEADERS ARE NOT PERSONS WHO DO THINGS RIGHT BUT THE ONES WHO FIND THE RIGHT THINGS TO DO.

Effective leaders also know that when they put people first, their effectiveness and efficiency improve. Their effective leadership enables them to get things done through people. The story is told of a little boy who valiantly but futilely tried to move a heavy log to clear a pathway to his favorite hideout. His father stood nearby and finally asked him why he wasn't using all his strength. The little boy assured his dad that he was straining with all his might. His dad quietly informed his son, "You are not using all your strength because you did not ask me to help."

Effective leaders use all their strength by recognizing, developing, and utilizing the physical, mental, and spiritual talents of those whom they lead. They learn what motivates others, and they transfer their own feelings of excitement and enthusiasm to those who follow their leadership. Here are a few distinguished historical leaders:

Julius Caesar, a great Roman general and statesman, was born Laius Julius Caesar on July 12, 100 BC. He was the most famous of Roman names and was described as being mighty, bold, royal, and loving. He was a man of infinite versatility, perhaps the most gifted man in Roman history. His early performance in the courts showed that he could have been a brilliant barrister had he chosen such a career. He possessed self-confidence, and in the face of hardship and difficulty, his troops trusted and believed in him.

Sir Winston Churchill, an English statesman and writer, was born in Blenheim Palace, Oxfordshire, England, on November 30, 1874. He entered the British Army as a subaltern in the Fourth Hussars in 1895 and participated in the Spanish campaign against Cuban insurrectionists as a correspondent. In 1900, at the age of twenty-five, Churchill was elected to parliament for Oldham as a conservative. In 1908, he became president of the Board of Trade; in 1910, he was Home Secretary; and in 1911, he was made first lord of the admiralty. Churchill was twice Prime Minister of England. During a time of war, he furnished the British people with relentless and inspiring leadership.

Dr. Martin Luther King Jr., an American Clergyman and militant, was a nonviolent Civil rights leader of the 1950s and 1960s. He was instrumental in introducing the strategy of civil disobedience to the black struggle for equality, and he turned the struggle into a mass movement. Dr. King was born in Atlanta, Georgia, in January 1929, the son of a Baptist minister.

He was an excellent student who entered Morehouse College in Atlanta at the age of fifteen and graduated with honors in 1948 at age nineteen. He graduated first in his class at Crozer Theological Seminary in Pennsylvania in 1951 and received a PhD in theology from Boston University In 1955. Rosa Parks, a black woman in the South, was arrested in December 1955 for refusing to move to the back of a public bus in Montgomery, Alabama. Blacks responded with a year-long bus boycott, and Dr. King, the president of the Montgomery Improvement Association, helped lead the protest.

In January 1957, Dr. King became one of the founders of the Southern Christian Leadership Conference that coordinated many civil rights organizations. He was involved in the sit-ins and freedom rides of 1960 and 1961 and was often jailed. In October 1964, Dr. King was awarded the Nobel Peace Prize for his nonviolent struggle against racial oppression. On April 4, 1968, he was assassinated in Memphis, Tennessee. He had led millions of people into shattering forever the Southern system of segregation of the races. Above all, Dr. Martin Luther King Jr. brought a newer and higher dimension of human dignity to black people's lives.

I am sure you are wondering why I have shared so much old history. Well, my point is that I would like for you to consider each of these leaders being different in scope, power, and position—each from a different era: one a soldier, one a statesman, and the other a civil rights leader. Each being different yet possessing essentially the same qualities of leadership. All were unusual, bold, self-confident, and courageous. They were men who were not afraid to dance to the tune of a different drummer, and in the case of Dr. Martin Luther King, Jr., he was one with a deep commitment to helping his fellow human beings.

True leadership carries responsibilities, love, truth, and courage to do what is right. Dr. King said, "An individual has not started living until he can rise above the narrow confines of his individualistic concerns to the broader concerns of all humanity." He also said, "Everybody can be great because anybody can serve. You don't have to have a college degree to serve. You don't have to make your subject and your verb agree to serve. You don't have to know Einstein's theory of relativity to serve. You don't have to know the second theory of thermodynamics in physics to serve. You only need a heart full of grace, a soul generated by love."

Leadership Uniqueness

Leaders must have a vision because they believe it's what they're supposed to do or that they may avoid a vision because they believe it has no real value. Stephen Covey describes vision as "seeing the end from the beginning." A vision is a mental image or a direction or goal of the future.

Sometimes leaders think that everyone expects them to settle on a vision alone. Some single-handedly visualize their organization's future while others work with their team to willingly determine the future state of readiness. Creating the vision together develops unity and commitment.

Your success and your children's future success or failure depends largely upon the ability to absorb facts, skills, and procedures and how to use them. Our brain stores the information it receives in an organized fashion, which makes it easier for our mind to comprehend and retain what we receive. We can help our brain to comprehend and retain this information by organizing the flow of the information. Any idea, word, phrase, or sentence can be turned into a question just by placing one of these six words in front.

1. Who?
2. What?
3. Where?
4. When?
5. Why?
6. How?

You should memorize these valuable words. They can help you in remembering information from newspapers and magazines. Journalists and some authors are trained to write using these six questions to arrange and organize text.

Wisdom is an important leadership trait that some leaders might not appreciate. Leaders must apply wisdom to their accumulated knowledge. They become more knowledgeable over time as they learn to discern reality from fantasy. Some people tend to follow individuals whom they believe to be wise. The wise leader gets to what is really important in dealing with life's difficult challenges.

Vince Lombardi, legendary football coach, once said, "The quality of people's lives is in direct proportion to their commitment to excellence, regardless of their field of endeavor." Leaders must inspire people to commit to be their best rather than complying with minimal performance standards.

People commit themselves to a team or organization when they believe their leaders value them and the best they have to offer. They need to know that their best matters. The leader's challenge is to show them that it does.

Exceptional leaders are known for the competence they've acquired in some field of endeavor. Their proficiency normally includes a relatively high degree of technical knowledge in their chosen profession. More importantly, they realize that it's their ability to achieve goals through the competency of others that defines them as an effective leader. These leaders are comfortable with what they know and don't know.

Proficiency among leaders is the ability to inspire, develop, support, reward, and reinforce people in the organized quest for a worthy end. Competent leaders recognize that success is not about them; it's about the people they lead. They understand their own strengths and use them for the good of the organization.

Competent leaders demonstrate openness to new ideas that may initially appear to contradict existing beliefs. They give the assurance that the organization has a clear and compelling vision of the future.

Dwight Eisenhower said, "Motivation is the art of getting people to do what you want them to do because they want to do it." Effective leaders push others to accomplish goals by overcoming their obstacles. They consistently display positive inspiration by setting an example others want to follow. These leaders help others aspire to the finest in themselves, including a belief in their abilities. They focus individual and group efforts on goals worth reaching, challenging themselves and those around them to work together for the common good. When the going gets rough, motivational leaders remain calm and positive, keeping themselves and those around them on track toward their destination.

Leadership is about persistence as much as it is about talent. Leaders who create a legacy are not those whose paths are organized but have completed missions with trials.

Whether you were born a leader or trained to be one, consistently radiate the will to go around, through, over, or under the obstacles on your path. No matter how many or how intimidating the challenges between you and a goal, leaders never quit. Perseverance is a defining quality of your leadership legacy.

Communication is the recurrent process through which leaders exchange ideas, feelings, knowledge, and information to build relationships of trust and respect.

Effective leaders communicate both to share their perspectives and to understand the views of others. They build trust and respect by demonstrating interest beyond themselves and their own agendas. This "give and take" works best when people interact face-to-face in an environment where all views are respectfully sought, heard, and understood.

People expect their leaders to remain composed, calm, and steady, particularly in times of tension or crisis. Even the most passionate leaders must exhibit steady, reassuring behavior when pressing circumstances make self-control difficult. Composure means keeping a level head, focusing on what needs to be done, and preventing emotions from overwhelming the organization's guiding principles, competence, and common sense.

The composed leaders project confidence; even when they are not feeling confident, they become a calming influence. When unsure, leaders must display faith in their ability and that of their team to succeed. Such composure might be the glue that keeps the team together and functioning.

Courage is a trait that leaders must exhibit in their own lives along with the lives of others. Whether it's long-standing or newly discovered, courage is the ability to press forward through all fears and doubts toward a worthy goal. It is an essential characteristic of leaders. People tend to follow individuals who display the courage to overcome obstacles. You can build up courage by understanding your fears then putting them into perspective by measuring them against the value of the goal you seek to lead others to achieve. Courage is moving forward despite your fears.

Nothing demonstrates greater respect and authentic interest in others than listening to recognize their needs, concerns, and views. Leaders must focus only on the truly important, thus setting aside the less important. Stephen Covey describes this prioritization process as "putting first things first."

Resist the temptation to elevate the priority of less-important, seemingly urgent matters beyond their real impact on your success. This leadership ability is essential. Without focus, individuals and organizations lose their way.

Discipline is important to leadership. You must discipline yourself to listen carefully so you can build the trust that enables you to be an effective leader.

Character is the foundation for leaders to win respect. By constant self-discipline and self-control, they can develop character, which is an extension of their values. *Merriam-Webster* defines character as the way someone thinks, feels, and behaves; someone's personality; a set of qualities that are shared by many people in a group, country, etc.; a set of qualities that make a place or thing different from other places or things.

Character is a component of true success. There is no single path to fulfillment of character, for everyone has different passions and needs. Character involves the attributes of integrity, values, credibility, honesty, kindness, sincerity, patience; being focused, hardworking, and passionate.

Success is defined by the principle of integrity. It is one thing to understand the components of true success. Living success involves action, conviction, and self-knowledge—commodities that you alone can supply. Ultimately, our success is based on our personal integrity and *values*. These principles enable us to maintain our self-respect no matter the circumstances.

In healthy organizations, values are alive. When actions run counter to the organization's values, havoc persists. Our values are known by the amount of time, attention, resources, and reinforcement that we give to our beliefs.

Credibility is essential to developing a reputation for personal integrity. It is one of the fundamental attributes of effective leaders. Credibility is built with others over time by consistently doing what we say we will do. Maintaining an unbreakable link between our actions and words doesn't mean people will always agree with us. It means people can rely on us to do as we say and believe. The attribute of credibility takes time to build, but it can be lost in a moment when our actions don't match our words.

People have faith in honest leaders. They do not expect their leaders to be perfect, but they do want to know that their word is truth. This is how trust is built, which is crucial to leaders not being perceived as lying, cheating, or stealing. Their character is built upon morals. Leaders cannot attain trust needed to build a vision without honesty.

Kindness matters; it is essential to helping followers feel good. It can also inspire them to want to be good and be a team player. Just one act of kindness can win the heart of people who lack motivation and self-esteem.

People want their leaders to be kind to them when providing feedback on their professional development and when conducting job interviews. Being honest can help people grow in areas that they might not have known needed improvement. Leaders must never be too busy to take time in giving eye-to-eye contact when sharing honest feedback in the workplace or in personal relationships.

Patience has contributed to many great leadership successes. Gandhi demonstrated extraordinary patience in working for a free and independent India. For more than thirty years, he was committed to nonviolence. His patience resulted in a free India. His patience was attributed to his success.

A lack of patience in leadership can cause national and international chaos and disaster especially in the area of investments and financial affairs. Everyone wants immediate feedback, not realizing the duration of some projects and commitments. Our ability to lead with patience requires clarity of vision and goals, so people can know where they are going and the projected time it takes to attain certain goals. If they know that some results are long term, then they can plan accordingly and not be surprised when nothing happens overnight or in the immediate future.

Effective leadership requires having a focus on the internal and external affairs of an organization, which can improve their ability to strategize and manage their organization. While we focus on ourselves, we have to be aware of others around us and in the world. The big picture should always be at the forefront of our mind, so we can be able to utilize today's technology and social media. Being focused in leadership is a task that requires us to direct our attention where it is needed while being able to recognize things that are a distraction.

It is said that some of the best leaders work harder than the people they lead. Nothing can replace hard work no matter how many degrees or experience. There comes a time when leaders need to know how to get out of their offices and become immersed in the workplace. There is a big difference from looking through a glass window than being able to have a hands-on approach. Making connections with the people you lead can give you a better understanding of their job descriptions on paper and the reality of their work.

Passionate leadership is an essential quality in leaders. It is sometimes hard to describe, but you know passion when you see it. Passion drives leaders to go over and beyond the call of duty. They see the company as their own, and they lead as though they bought it. They are constantly looking around to see what and how they can make improvements to the vision and its surroundings. Passionate leadership demonstrates positive and optimistic views; the leaders are determined to do their best to make the company succeed. They will always give more than 100 percent in their continuous efforts to set the tone for their subordinates.

ACRONYMS

LEADERSHIP ACCOUNTABILITY IN GOVERNMENT

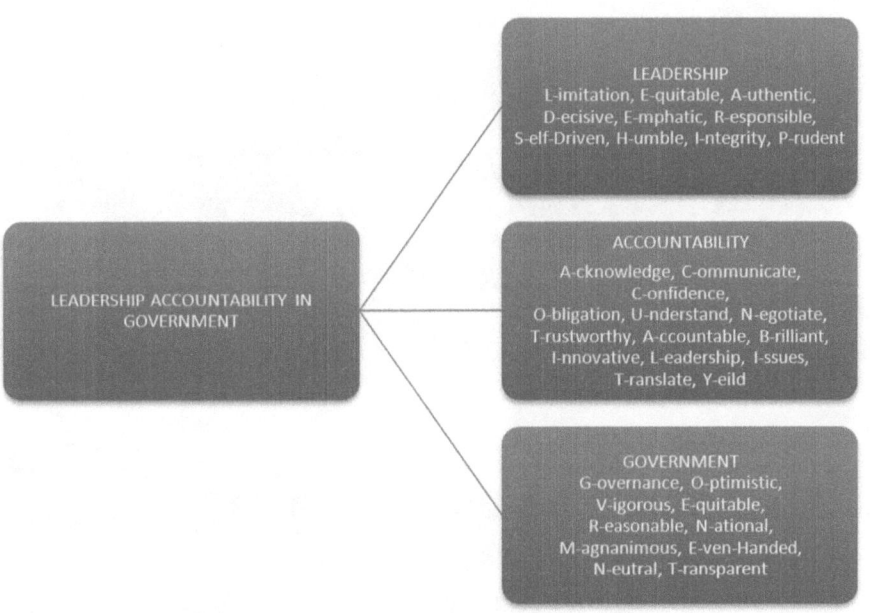

LEADERSHIP ACCOUNTABILITY IN GOVERNMENT

LEADERSHIP
L-imitation, E-quitable, A-uthentic, D-ecisive, E-mphatic, R-esponsible, S-elf-Driven, H-umble, I-ntegrity, P-rudent

ACCOUNTABILITY
A-cknowledge, C-ommunicate, C-onfidence, O-bligation, U-nderstand, N-egotiate, T-rustworthy, A-ccountable, B-rilliant, I-nnovative, L-eadership, I-ssues, T-ranslate, Y-eild

GOVERNMENT
G-overnance, O-ptimistic, V-igorous, E-quitable, R-easonable, N-ational, M-agnanimous, E-ven-Handed, N-eutral, T-ransparent

CHAPTER 2

Accountability Framework

Although the business of government has changed over the years, government reporting continues to focus heavily on inputs, process, and compliance, not on outcomes, and is primarily concerned with financial accountability. Even though some government organizations have shifted their emphasis to the management of results, public accountability for results has not fully followed suit.

Many jurisdictions do not have a conceptual framework for defining and reporting on performance across the spectrum of government activities. A comprehensive accountability framework should be developed to guide all levels of governing. The framework should be integrated with government's performance management processes, such as strategic planning and budget and expenditure control. It should address the following:

What Is Accountability?

Accountability is the obligation to account for responsibilities conferred. It is a concept fundamental to a democratic system, and it clearly establishes the right of the citizen to know what government intends to achieve on behalf of its citizens and how well it has met its intentions. In The Bahamas, it means that government is accountable to the Legislative Assembly for the way in which it manages the power and resources entrusted to it. In turn, the Legislative Assembly, on behalf of the people, is responsible for ensuring that this accountability takes place.

Who Is Accountable to Whom?

Accountability should be required at all levels of governing, from the individual employee to the program level, from the program level to the corporate level, from the corporate level to the government level, and from the government level to the Legislative Assembly, on behalf of the people.

Accountability should also be comprehensive in its scope—that is, it should apply to ministries, Crown corporations, and funded agencies (such as regional health boards and school boards), and to government as a whole.

In a parliamentary system of government, accountability is exercised through several levels. It begins at the societal level, where the long-range goals for members of society are generally understood. These goals are typically broad in nature, such as encouraging a robust economy or ensuring that citizens are healthy and productive, but are generally not articulated. How these goals will be carried out is determined at the ballot box when citizens approve the objectives and strategies that a particular political party intends to use to achieve these societal goals. However, it is possible that these goals can be formalized, thereby forming the basis for accountability.

At the next level, governments develop their strategies for achieving specific objectives in support of the broad societal goals. These objectives and strategies may be part of a strategic plan and tend to coincide with the number of years that a government is in office. To carry out its administration over this period, the government is provided with its power and resources by the Legislative Assembly on behalf of the people. In return, the government is accountable to the assembly for the way in which it has discharged its administration. In practice, ministers carry out accountability individually during a question period and the estimates debates on government spending by members of legislative committees and through the tabling of annual reports and other documents before the Legislative Assembly. Such an arrangement reflects government's organization into Ministries, Crown corporations, and funded agencies, and ensures that the assembly receives a direct accounting from the minister responsible for each organization.

At the corporate level are the ministries, public corporations, and funded agencies that carry out the government's strategies for achieving its objectives. These individual organizations plan their corporate activities for the medium term, ideally linking their plans to societal and government objectives. Activities at the corporate level generally include the preparation of business plans, spending commitments, and annual reports. Accountability flows from the board members of public corporations and the parliamentary secretaries within government to the responsible minister who, in turn, is accountable to the parliament.

At the program level, organizational objectives are translated into action through the planning and delivery of public programs and services. Ideally, program managers are held accountable for the results achieved by these programs and services as well as compliance with input controls and administrative regulations. Accountability is exercised up the line to the Minister of State or board members of Crown corporations. However, it is also at the program level where citizens most directly judge the impact that government is having on their lives.

Accountability does not end at the program level. Individual public sector employees are also responsible for the way in which they plan and carry out their assigned tasks and may be held accountable by way of performance targets and regular performance assessments.

Many programs are delivered indirectly through funded agencies such as regional health boards, school boards, colleges, and universities. Although these organizations receive public funds from government, they are not directly accountable to the Legislative Assembly. Government, however, through its ministers, must ensure that funded agencies are responsible in the way they use public funds. Citizens pay for results and expect to be informed as to what has been achieved by all of government on their behalf.

What Is Government Accountable For?

Government should be clear about its intentions, objectives, and strategies; the costs of its strategies; and the actual results achieved. Ideally, such information would be based on an effective performance management system. This includes having in place clear objectives, effective strategies, aligned management systems, performance measurement reporting, and real consequences.

Historically, governments have reported on financial accountability, including compliance with spending authorities. This information continues to be important, particularly given concerns about the debt and deficit, but government is responsible for much more. It has an obligation to make program choices and deliver these programs and services in the best interests of its citizens. These decisions go beyond financial considerations to include issues such as fairness and equity. At the same time, the citizens who support or use these programs want to know that government is actually achieving what it intended to; that money is being spent wisely; that they are getting value for money for their tax dollars; and that government is conducting its business in a fair, legal, and ethical manner.

To understand such issues, legislators and citizens need to know what government intends to achieve and why, and what it has actually achieved and how. In turn, the government must be clear about its objectives and targets, the strategies it will employ to meet its objectives, the full costs of these strategies, and its actual results. To be accountable, it should explain if and why its results differed from what was intended and what action it took. Information such as this would be derived from a management system geared for results.

Levels of Accountability

Although accountability flows from the individual employees to program managers, senior executives, ministers, and the Legislative Assembly, citizens are interested in the results achieved at various levels of accountability. As service recipients, customers, taxpayers, or members of special interest groups, they want to know how government has served their interests.

Within a parliamentary system of government, the lines of accountability seem clear: public servants are accountable to ministers, ministers are accountable to the Legislative Assembly (MLA), and they are accountable to the people by means of elections. In practice, though, accountability is not as simple as this.

As governments have grown in size and complexity, the principle of ministerial responsibility requires examination. While ministers are clearly responsible for policy, many people question the practicality of holding them to account for the day-to-day management of their administrations. Furthermore, as the breadth and depth of government becomes so far-reaching, it is clear that many objectives can no longer be achieved by any one minister.

Another issue of accountability concerns the collective responsibility of ministers. As members of Cabinet and Cabinet committees, ministers not only formulate priorities and broad policies of government, they are also responsible for overseeing government-wide management systems that bring about those priorities and policies. Under the Financial Administration and Audit Act 1973, for example, the financial management of government is entrusted not to an individual minister but to a committee of the Cabinet. It could be argued that ministers have a collective as well as an individual responsibility to account to the Legislative Assembly and through it to the people for the performance of government.

What Information Should Be Reported?

Accountability information should encompass the range of a government's activities. For its financial performance, information is required on the use and source of funds, financial results, and financial integrity. For its legal compliance and its fairness, equity, and probity, information is required on the extent to which government has met its legislative requirements and its standards of conduct such as its human rights, employment equity, and conflict of interest. For its organizational and program performance, information is required on the relevance and responsiveness of programs, the appropriateness of programs, and the program results, such as outcomes, outputs, acceptance, and secondary impacts, and management results such as management direction, working environment, and the monitoring and reporting systems.

Various types of information can be made available to the Legislative Assembly for the range of government activities. Program performance, for example, can be described in annual reports by providing information about actual results compared to program objectives and performance targets. Similarly, the total expenditures of a ministry can be compared to its voted appropriation to give readers an understanding of the ministry's financial results. Such a comparison is already made in the public accounts of the government.

How Much Information Should Be Provided?

The type of information and the level of detail to be provided will vary according to the level of governing. For example, at the program level in the health field, program managers may want to know hospital bed utilization rates; at the government level, legislators and taxpayers may want to know how the decision to locate a facility was made; and at the societal level, legislators and citizens may want to know what the health goals are for the local government. We believe the information needed to answer these and similar questions are the same as that required for effective management. However, the information would need to be aggregated differently. Program managers, for instance, would likely require more detailed information than legislators would need to assess government performance.

What Should the Quality of That Information Be?

The quality of the information to be reported is critical if it is to be of value in assessing performance. Accountability information should be relevant (deal with matters of interest to users); complete (deal with all significant aspects of financial and nonfinancial data of the subject matter); meaningful (be readily comparable to previous periods, provide sufficient contextual material, and be presented in a readily understandable way); fair (fairly represent in tone and balance the underlying information); timely (available to users in time for it to be of value in assessing performance and making decisions); accessible (be provided through a medium that is readily usable); consistent (be reported in the same manner over time); and verifiable (be capable of independent checking or auditing).

How Should the Information Be Verified?

As broader accountability information is produced, the quality of the information that is reported, and possibly the measures that are used, should be independently verified. An audit methodology may need to be developed and tested for public accountability.

How Should Accountability Information Be Provided?

No single report can meet the accountability requirement of the government to the Legislative Assembly; a variety of reports are needed. Summary reports can provide important information at the government-wide level. Sectoral reports, such as the *Report on the State of the Environment*, can provide valuable information about the status of a particular policy area; organizational reports can provide more detailed information about the operations of government programs. The information to be reported will vary in detail according to the level of accountability. Accountability information could be made available electronically, as well as in print, as a way of reducing costs and broadening accessibility.

When Should Accountability Information Be Provided?

Performance information should be reported regularly, through the various levels of accountability, to the Legislative Assembly. Depending on the needs of the assembly, information may be required quarterly, annually, or periodically.

Chapter 3

Accountability in Government

Simply reporting to the parliament is not enough. If the assembly is to hold government to account, it must inform itself about what government intends and what government achieves.

What Should the Legislative Assembly Do with the Information It Receives?

The Legislative Assembly's Role in Accountability

In a parliamentary system of government, citizens have a right to know how they are being governed. This right of accountability is exercised, in the interests of the people, by the elected representatives of the Legislative Assembly. If the assembly is to understand what government intends to achieve on behalf of its citizens and how well it has met its intentions, Members of Legislative Assembly (MLAs) need to be informed. This means that the Legislative Assembly should receive meaningful information and should use it actively to judge the performance of government.

In The Bahamas, government and opposition members alike have acknowledged the need for improved accountability. A key question for legislators is whether programs are achieving the outcomes they were intended to achieve and doing so with the greatest efficiency. To answer this question, legislators have suggested that what is needed is a comprehensive picture of program performance—that is, meaningful information about results achieved compared to the results expected.

In calling for accountability for results, the assembly may want to define, in explicit terms, the information it requires to assess the performance of government. It is suggested that such information should include the intentions and actual results of a government's activities—that is, the financial performance, legal compliance and fairness, equity and probity, and organizational and program performance. A fair and complete assessment of this performance would extend beyond a government's ministries to include other government organizations and enterprises, most of which are Crown corporations.

This is an important point because Crown corporations are a vital part of the public sector in The Bahamas. Over the years, Crown corporations were either established or acquired by government to provide a range of services for its citizens: electricity, transport, automobile insurance, rental housing, and trade development, for example. For many of these corporations, the government provides financial assistance and guarantees their debt. Several corporations are also funded annually by appropriations from the Consolidated Revenue Fund or have been given the power to raise their own revenue.

For Crown corporations, it is the Legislative Assembly that performs many of the functions associated with ownership of private sector corporations. The assembly authorizes a corporation's creation, mandate, disposal, and dissolution, and provides the funds. Ultimately, it is to the Legislative Assembly, through the ministers responsible, that the Crown corporations owe their accountability.

It is critical, therefore, that the Legislative Assembly receives information on the performance of all of government, not just its ministries. Although, in practice, the government of the day will decide on the information to be reported, no government can operate without regard for the wishes of the assembly. It is clear that, in representing the people, the Legislative Assembly has primacy and ultimately its demands for accountability must prevail. The most powerful vehicle available to the assembly in this regard is legislation.

Legislative Committees

Legislative committees exist to allow Members of Parliament to carry out a more detailed analysis of matters than would be possible if such issues came before the assembly as a whole. Its members are chosen from among all parliamentarians and are empowered to call witnesses and examine documents. Legislative committees are expected to produce nonpartisan reports on issues referred to them and report directly to the parliament. Where a committee cannot reach agreement, the conclusions of the majority become the conclusions of the committee.

The Select Standing Committee on Public Accounts is an important body because it is responsible for seeing that public monies are applied for the purposes authorized by the Legislative Assembly. It has an interest, as well, in determining whether policy is carried out efficiently, effectively, and economically.

Matters most commonly referred to the committee are the public accounts, the auditor general's reports, and applications for the retention and disposal of government documents. The Select Standing Committee on Public Accounts also hears testimony concerning compliance with authorities and value-for-money audits from the Office of the Auditor General and various ministries.

The Select Standing Committee on Public Accounts is a key forum for holding government to account. Given its potential for assessing the performance of the public sector as a whole, we believe Members of Parliament may wish to consider such questions as the following:

- Are legislative committees effective in holding government to account?
- How can Members of Parliament ensure that legislative committees function as a useful tool for accountability?
- Should other legislative committees be regularly convened to consider the performance of the government's ministries, public corporations, and funded agencies?
- Would a sectoral, rather than organizational, approach be of value in assessing government performance?
- Is the coverage of government performance complete?
- Does it adequately cover the operations of public corporations as well as ministries?
- Should the performance of all ministries and public corporations be assessed? If not, what organizations or sectors should be given priority?
- Should a legislative committee actively pursue ministry accountability for funded agencies?
- Is government performance assessed in a systematic fashion?
- Should the performance of government organizations be systematically scrutinized?
- To allow a comparison of government intentions and results, should the financial and operational plans, and the annual reports of ministries and public corporations, be automatically referred to legislative committees?
- Is the scope of legislative committees adequate?

- Should legislative committees be authorized to review the past, current, and committed expenditures of government organizations?
- Should legislative committees be allowed to review other expenditures of government?
- Should the terms of reference of legislative committees be more explicit in this regard?
- Is the time available to legislative committees sufficient?
- Would accountability be better served if legislative committees could also meet when the parliament is not in session?
- Are there committee activities (such as document retention and disposal, for example) that can be handled in another way?

Challenges for Public Sector Institutions

Major changes to the world economy, a rapid expansion in the scope of government activities since the end of World War II, high population shifts through international and interisland migration, the effects of the aging baby boom generation on government program demands, and the fiscal legacy of sustained deficit financing over a lengthy period have all contributed to the creation of an atmosphere of uncertainty and anxiety, common to many jurisdictions.

A major symptom of this atmosphere is the perceived decline in the public confidence in governments and government institutions. There is a growing public sentiment that government programs generally are not delivering sufficient value for the tax dollars being spent. In addition, there is a feeling that many of the government's operations are accountable only to themselves and do not adequately respond to public criticism.

Ensuring that the government operates at a high level of performance and provides full accountability for that performance would enhance public confidence in government and its institutions. The nonpartisan involvement of Members of Parliament is fundamental to the successful implementation of measures to improve accountability as it is largely through the parliament that government is held accountable to the general public.

Accountability is a contract between two parties. In the case of government, the contract it has with the public is an implicit one in which the public gives government the responsibility to govern and manage public resources. In turn, the government is accountable to the public, through the legislature, for its performance. As such, the parliament has an essential role in assessing that performance.

The average citizens do not have a clear and comprehensive idea of how well their government is performing. Often the information citizens receive on government performance is through media stories on selected issues. While information on current issues and government programs is more readily available to Members of Parliament, it is often not available in a form useful for assessing the effectiveness of government policies and programs.

Also, key to improving accountability is securing a change in the way publicly funded bodies (including ministries, public corporations, and funded agencies such as regional health boards and school boards) plan, manage, and measure their performance. These bodies will have to shift from their present emphasis on management of program inputs to that of clearly identifying desired results and measuring performance against these objectives. Effective ways of reporting on program performance to the government, the legislature, and the public will also have to be developed.

Management processes also need to evolve to meet the new challenge. Roles and responsibilities should be defined and management systems, reporting systems, and, indeed, the prevailing management culture altered if real change is to be effected.

Today, the range of goods and services that government provides to the public is much wider, and the resulting benefits of those goods and services are less easily identified. This is a problem because, as fiscal pressures mount, government is being forced to reassess which programs to maintain and which to reduce or terminate—a job made difficult when results are unclear. Moreover, the public is now demanding an increased role in the development of public policy and programs.

There is a realization within the governments that they can no longer accumulate budget deficits and debt to provide services. In addition, the international financial community, bond investors, and bond rating agencies are exerting increasing pressure on governments to reduce or eliminate deficits. Governments also recognize that if confidence in government fiscal management is allowed to falter, this could translate into increased borrowing costs and then into declining borrowing power.

At the same time, increased global competition and major economic changes have caused the general public to experience a decline in real incomes, a decline that has reduced the acceptability of increased taxes. Public demand for service, nevertheless, has continued unabated. This is creating unprecedented pressures on governments to clarify public priorities, to refocus resources to these priorities, and to improve efficiency of programs.

The government must respond to these pressures by focusing on reducing or eliminating deficits. Many governments are attempting to meet reduced spending targets through a range of measures, including service reductions and withdrawal from activities no longer considered appropriate or essential. There is also a desire to identify and discontinue programs that

---

do not work well and to improve the relevance and efficiency of government programs that will be continued, demonstrating to the public that better value will be achieved for money spent.

These efforts are complicated by the fact that government has many different clients and constituencies to satisfy. The interests and demands of these groups are wide ranging and often conflicting; and any one individual can fall into several groups as, for example, a taxpayer, service recipient, employee, and program deliverer. Priorities can therefore change rapidly, depending on the perspective in force at any particular time.

Government Strategic Priorities

A government's strategic planning process should identify and articulate its goals and priorities over the term of its administration. Public involvement in setting direction and objectives should be a part of this process; it is an important aspect of accountability.

The minister of finance should give consideration to having annual budget consultations with members of the business and financial communities, labor organizations, and the community at large. This would significantly enhance the accountability process.

A significant effort should be made also to communicate the government's strategic plan throughout ministries, public corporations, and funded agencies. All ministries should be required to prepare strategic plans at the corporate level to guide their operations. These plans can be presented at annual financial planning conference held each year prior to the annual budget exercise.

Ministries and public corporations should manage for results. Their work needs to be coordinated and formally linked to the budget, strategic planning processes, and public reporting. Work done by ministries and funded agencies should be with a clearly articulated set of policy guidelines from the Treasury Department. In addition, the roles and responsibilities for central agencies, ministries, public corporations, and other government organizations, the auditor general, and the Legislative Assembly must be clearly defined.

Overview of the Accountabilities of the Free Trade Area of the Americas Process

The effort to unite the economies of the Western Hemisphere into a single free trade agreement began at the Summit of the Americas, which was held in December 1994 in Miami. The Heads of State and government of the thirty-four democracies in the region agreed to construct a Free Trade Area of the Americas, or FTAA, in which barriers to trade and investment will be progressively eliminated, and to complete negotiations for the agreement by 2005. The leaders also committed to achieve substantial progress toward building the FTAA by 2000. Their decisions are contained in the Miami Summit's Declaration of Principles and Plan of Action.

Four ministerial meetings took place during the preparatory phase of the FTAA process: the first was in June 1995 in Denver, USA; the second in March 1996 in Cartagena, Colombia; the third in May 1997 in Belo Horizonte, Brazil; and the fourth in March 1998 in San José, Costa Rica. At their meeting in San José, ministers recommended to their Heads of State and government the initiation of negotiations and set out the structure and general principles and objectives to guide the negotiations. On the basis of the San José Declaration, the FTAA negotiations were launched formally in April 1998 at the Second Summit of the Americas in Santiago, Chile. The leaders agreed that the FTAA negotiating process be transparent and take into account the differences in the levels of development and size of the economies in the Americas in order to facilitate full participation by all countries.

At the sixth ministerial meeting held in Buenos Aires and at the Third Summit of the Americas held in Quebec City in April 2001, a number of key decisions were made regarding the FTAA negotiations. Ministers received from the negotiating groups a draft text of the FTAA and, in an unprecedented move designed to increase the transparency of the process, recommended to their Heads of State and government to make this text publicly available. The draft FTAA agreement was made available to the public in all four official languages on July 3, 2001. Ministers also highlighted the need to foster dialogue with civil society, and the summaries of the second round of civil society submissions in response to the open invitation were an agreement to be placed on the FTAA website. Ministers reiterated the importance of the provision of technical assistance to smaller economies to facilitate their participation in the FTAA.

Deadlines were fixed for the conclusion and implementation of the FTAA agreement. Negotiations were to be concluded no later than January 2005; entry into force was sought as soon as possible thereafter, no later than December 2005. Deadlines were also set for the market access negotiations. Recommendations on the methods and modalities for tariff negotiations were completed by April 1, 2002, and tariff negotiations were initiated no later than May 15, 2002. A second version of the draft FTAA agreement was prepared during the third negotiating phase, which ended in October 2002 at the seventh ministerial meeting held in Ecuador.

The agreed principles guide the negotiations. These include, among others:

- Decisions will be taken by consensus.
- Negotiations will be conducted in a transparent manner.
- The FTAA will be consistent with WTO rules and disciplines and should improve upon these rules and disciplines wherever possible and appropriate.
- The FTAA will be a single unit (nothing is agreed until all is agreed).
- The FTAA can coexist with bilateral and subregional agreements, and countries may negotiate and accept the obligations of the FTAA individually or as members of a subregional integration group. Special attention will be given to the needs of the smaller economies.

The FTAA negotiations are carried out under an agreed structure that is member driven and ensures broad geographical participation. The chairmanship of the entire process, the site of the negotiations themselves, as well as the chairs and vice chairs of the various negotiating groups and other committees and groups all rotate among participating countries. Chairmanship of the negotiations rotates every eighteen months or at the conclusion of each ministerial meeting.

Terrorist Financing and Risks to Financial Institutions

The terrorist attacks caused enormous destruction in New York City. The losses included the direct costs of the destruction to lives and property, as well as cleanup, and the indirect costs of lost income brought about by business closings and related spending reductions. It was expected that some of the losses would be covered by payments from private insurance, emergency federal relief funds, and charitable contributions. Other losses, however, may never be recovered because some individuals and businesses may not have been insured or may not qualify for federal relief or charity.

Moreover, the state budget documents indicate that of the $8 billion budget officials said was for economic stimulus, $5 billion was an estimate of costs to support families and dislocated workers who are unemployed because of the overall economic uncertainty created by the terrorist attacks and to rebuild New York City and ensure New York's recovery from the events of September 11, 2001.

A financial institution that carries out a transaction knowing that the funds or property involved are owned or controlled by terrorists or terrorist organizations, or that the transaction is linked to or likely to be used in terrorist activity, may be committing a criminal offense under the laws of many jurisdictions. Such an offense may exist regardless of whether the assets involved in the transaction were the proceeds of criminal activity or were derived from lawful activity but intended for use in support of terrorism.

Regardless of whether the funds in a transaction are related to terrorists for the purposes of national criminal legislation, business relationships with such individuals, or other closely associated persons or entities could, under certain circumstances, expose a financial institution to significant reputational, operational, and legal risk. This risk is even more serious if the person or entity involved is later shown to have benefited from the lack of effective monitoring or willful blindness of a particular institution and thus was to carry out terrorist acts.

It is clear that these events have changed the way we do business forever, and this is a significant challenge for the government and an expensive undertaking to cope with these new and difficult challenges.

CHAPTER 4

Elements of Effective Performance Management

Information to be reported at the government level should build on the information required for managing at the program level. However, the degree of details and the way the information is aggregated differs at each level of accountability.

To assess government performance fairly, legislators and the public need information about the intended and actual results for the range of government activity. Therefore, government should report publicly about the following:

Organizational and Program Performance

Government should show whether taxpayers are receiving the best possible value for money from government operations. It must be able to say whether the programs it delivers are the following:

1) relevant—that they make sense in relation to the problems they are designed to solve;
2) effective—that they achieve the intended results; and
3) efficient—that they achieve those results in the most economical and cost-effective manner.

Government should also be able to say whether its organizations have the capacity to deliver results in the future.

Management direction to staff should be clear and well understood, and staff should be well trained and qualified to meet the demands of the organization or program.

Financial Performance

Government should say whether it achieved its financial objectives and managed its financial affairs according to sound financial controls. Information about financial objectives includes

1) comparing actual revenues and expenditures to budgeted amounts;
2) comparing actual deficit to budgeted deficit; and
3) reporting on progress compared to the debt management plan.

Legal Compliance and Fairness, Equity, and Probity

Government and public service must report on how well they have met standards of behavior in the conduct of government business. This includes complying with the legislation and regulations governing the activities of government organizations. Areas that should be covered are human rights, employment standards, employment equity, conflict of interest, working conditions, and environmental safety; and meeting high standards of conduct and treating equitably employees, clients, suppliers, and other parties to government operations.

Setting Objectives and Measuring Performance

A key aspect of the public sector reforms has been a shift from compliance with rules and control of inputs to setting of clear objectives and measuring of results to translate the strategies into measurable goals or "benchmarks."

Benchmarks are designed to track overall progress toward goals rather than to measure specific program efforts to achieve those goals. Some benchmarks set targets and measure progress toward specific objectives, such as improving the readiness of young children for school; other benchmarks measure aspects of life that need to be maintained, such as housing affordability. The state's progress in meeting its strategic goals has been reported regularly to the legislature and the Bahamian people since 1973 with the Financial Administration and Audit Act.

Performance measures are considered a valuable tool, not only in demonstrating what is being accomplished with tax dollars but also in managing government programs. Monitoring trends in performance, comparing these measures to established policy targets or other relevant benchmarks, and governments should routinely perform taking action to alter unfavorable results. But, as well, given the public's increasing skepticism about the quality and cost effectiveness of government services, information about results is critical.

Reporting on Results

Government has a responsibility to report to the parliament and its citizens as to how well it has achieved the goals it has set out. The Bahamas have been required by legislation to report regularly on their progress in meeting the performance targets set for them.

In the United Kingdom, the key targets of executive agencies are published so that parliament, the public, customers, and staff can determine what each agency is expected to achieve. Information about each agency's performance, including the achievement of its key performance targets, is available in its annual report.

In New Zealand, each department must include a statement of objectives and a statement of service performance in its financial statements.

Legislators, in turn, can use performance information such as this to regularly monitor progress against a government's goals. Accountability information can serve as an early warning, not only for the government but also for the legislature, when policies or programs are not working. A report card has little value if its only purpose is to track our decline on important indicators. It is crucial for the legislature not only to take an interest in the performance of government but also to ensure that it has the capacity to use the information that is provided to it.

Making a Legislative Commitment

Many of these jurisdictions have also passed legislation establishing public accountability standards for reporting on the results achieved. Such legislation signals a legislature's interest in performance and serves to motivate program managers to pursue changes they might otherwise not pursue. However, many agree that simply passing laws is not enough. If government is not committed to the changes it purports to seek through its legislation, it may not gain the widespread support of its public sector management.

Performance Management in the Public Sector

Many citizens have been calling for improved accountability in their nation's public sector. Citizens want to know the intentions and actual results of government efforts and that accountability, as it is currently practiced, does not meet this need. This view does not reflect on any particular administration but, rather, recognizes that accountability practices that have evolved over many years have not kept pace with changing circumstances and expectations.

To meet the public's demands for improved performance and accountability, government must begin to change the way they plan, implement, and manage programs and service delivery. Over the past several years, many improvements in performance measurement and reporting have been made in various government ministries. There is a need now to focus on results—seeking clear objectives, developing effective strategies, and monitoring and reporting on performance. Many ministries and other public sector agencies are reviewing their planning, budgeting, and other management systems to more effectively deliver services to the public.

I am particularly conscious of the challenges inherent in developing and implementing a comprehensive performance management and accountability framework. It will take time and will require further improvements to management systems in government.

The business of government has evolved over many years so that today governments are involved in many aspects of a citizen's life. At the same time, public information about governments' activities has remained focused on issues of probity, prudence, and compliance with spending authorities. This is now changing, however, with the public wanting to know what their governments intend to achieve and why and what they have actually achieved and how. But little information is available about government objectives and results for the range of its activities—particularly organizational and program performance.

This is not unusual; many jurisdictions in the Caribbean and the Commonwealth of Nations and elsewhere are in a similar position and have begun to examine accountability in terms of government results rather than in terms of inputs, processes, and compliance.

Accountability for results is critical, not only to legislators in assessing government performance but also to government itself in managing its programs and services on behalf of the public. Consequently, the auditor general should meet with senior public sector executives and hold discussions with Members of Parliament from all parties.

I believe an effective accountability framework requires that government be clear about both its intended and actual results. Therefore, the framework should be closely integrated with a performance management system that includes the following:

- clear objectives
- effective strategies
- aligned management systems
- performance measurement and reporting
- real consequences for the success or failure of programs

This information should cover the range of government activities to allow an assessment of its financial performance; its legal compliance and fairness, equity, and probity; and its organizational and program performance. Of course, the type of information and level of detail to be provided would vary according to the level of accountability, but it would be based on the same information a government requires for effective management.

The information reported should be required to meet certain basic criteria, such as the following:

- relevant
- complete
- timely
- verifiable

Since no single report can serve the accountability interests of everyone, a variety of reports may be necessary.

- Summary-level reports are useful at the government-wide level.
- Sectoral reports provide valuable information about the status of particular policy areas of government such as environment.
- Organizational reports provide more detailed information about the operations of government programs.
- Performance information contained in these reports should be reported regularly to the parliament.

It should be noted that the role of Members of Parliament is fundamental to accountability because it is largely through the parliament that government is held accountable to the people for its performance. The needs of the parliament are, therefore, critical in designing an appropriate accountability framework.

CHAPTER 5

Toward Greater Accountability in Government

Where Do We Begin?

The issue of accountability in government has been one of the most topical subjects among the nations. There has been greater awareness and demands for greater parliamentary scrutiny and accountability on all bodies receiving public funds.

Constitutional and Legislative Basis of Government

Audit: The Mandate

The auditor general is an important link in the chain of accountability. The primary element of accountability as seen by a public sector manager may well be to the government, but the final accountability must be to parliament on behalf of their constituents—"the people." As a result, not only does the auditor general have a much better base on which to work but, more importantly, is now required to provide the assurance to parliament and the public that is inherent in the auditor general's opinion on all aspects of the organization's activities. This would set the stage for an effective value-for-money auditing program.

The Concept: Components and Characteristics

Value-for-money auditing basically is a concept that is based on two important principles of management in the public sector.

The First Principle

The first principle states that public business should be conducted in a way that makes the best possible use of public funds. Officials responsible for spending public funds must ensure that their decisions are "legal and ethical." They must ensure that these decisions result in economical, efficient, and effective public services of appropriate amounts at appropriate times and at the best price. Resources, people, goods, and money should be used as productively as possible; and programs should achieve their intended results. In other words, good decisions in the public sector are those that not only are legal and ethical but also reflect value for money.

The Second Principle

The second principle states that people who conduct public business should be accountable for the prudent and effective management of the resources entrusted to them. This onus of accountability permeates the whole of the public sector, from elected representatives who are accountable to the public officials who are accountable to elected and public service superiors. At every level, there is an obligation to demonstrate that good management practices are being followed.

The principle of accountability applies to all public servants at all levels within public sector organizations. Therefore, the concept of value-for-money auditing is as applicable to "internal auditing for management's use" as it is to external auditing done for elected and governing bodies and the public.

Value-for-money does not confine itself to examining the past. It uses its analysis of existing controls, "information systems," and reporting practices to recommend improvements designed to result in greater economy, efficiency, and effectiveness.

The specific techniques used in the conduct of value-for-money audits will vary from one audit to another. Value-for-money auditing is not a technique but rather a concept to help auditors of public-funded organizations decide what they should examine and report on and a framework to help them do it.

Definition

A comprehensive value-for-money audit is an examination that provides an "objective and constructive" assessment of the extent to which financial, human and physical resources are managed with due regard to economy and efficiency and effectiveness and accountability relationships are reasonably served.

The value-for-money audit examines both financial and management controls, including information systems and reporting practices, and it recommends improvements where appropriate. Certain aspects of this definition merit elaboration. The idea of "accountability" relationship is crucial. It is based on the assumption that those who confer responsibility should expect and should receive an appropriate accounting for the discharge of responsibilities conferred.

The value-for-money audit "concept" focuses on and deals with accountability relationships in two ways:

1) It examines the clarity of understanding that exists about who the principal parties are in these relationships and how the responsibility to provide for proper accountability is to be discharged.
2) It examines how in practice this responsibility is discharged by those who manage public funds.

However, it is not the function of the auditor general to attempt to prescribe what the accountability relationships ought to be within an organization. That is the job and prerogative of the elected and appointed officials involved. Nonetheless, the accountability relationships may be clarified and strengthened as a result of the value-for-money audit examination. In formulating an ideal set of procedures to implement this new state of the art auditing, I recognize however that there is a gap between what is desirable and what is practical, from the point of cost and usefulness.

I further recognize that there is no universal formula for defining the kind of information that public officials need to discharge their responsibilities; the test of "reasonableness" is the only one available. Accordingly, while certain types of information might improve accountability, the value-for-money or performance auditing concept recognizes that the cost of obtaining that information must be weighed against its potential benefits.

Characteristic: Basic Auditing Standards

Generally understood and accepted attributes of traditional financial auditing evidence, due care, fair reporting, and independence, are equally essential to value-for-money audits. The presence of these attributes ensures that the audit report is objective and reliable, prepared independently of those who are responsible for the program or activity under review and based upon a disciplined examination of appropriate evidence.

The credibility of a value-for-money audit is dependent in large part on the professionalism of those undertaking it and therefore on the independence and objectivity with which they approach their task.

Comprehensive

Breadth and scope are the characteristics that clearly distinguish value-for-money auditing from the traditional financial auditing. At the planning stage, value-for-money audits will now identify all the major activities, controls, and systems of the public sector organizations and select those among them who are essential to the judicious use of the organization's resources. These are then subject to a comprehensive audit. It implies a conscious and systematic process at the beginning of the audit to understand the entire organization including its structure, key activities, broad control needs, and the type of information that legislators, members of the governing bodies, and/or senior executives and managers have available to them. This form of comprehensive planning will now be the key to focusing the audit effort on the most critical areas and issues. It can easily then be recognized that value-for-money auditing does not imply a wall-to-wall examination of all activities, controls, and systems; such broad audits, from my point of view, would be costly, disruptive, difficult to control, or of doubtful cost effectiveness.

The terms *efficiency*, *effectiveness*, and *economy* which characterize value-for-money audits, do not imply that an organization's entire structure of programs and units need to be audited simultaneously. Instead, the audit can be conducted on a selective piece-by-piece basis over a designated period of time. It is a characteristic of value-for-money auditing that the major activities, systems, procedures, and controls of an organization are usually examined over the course of several audits, thereby creating an audit cycle within an organization. This approach recognizes that it would probably be unproductive to repeat detailed examinations of the same aspects of the same organizational unit year after year.

The actual length of the audit cycle will be determined by such factors as the following:

- the size and complexity of the organization
- the resources devoted to audit

- the amount of change the organization is experiencing
- the extent to which key systems can be relied on to ensure continued regard for value-for-money auditing are likely to be achieved, only if there is a spirit of cooperation and interest among all parties throughout the process from planning through to making whatever improvements are warranted.

There should be an ongoing dialogue between the audit personnel and all parties in the accountability relationship; because of the very nature of value-for-money auditing, at the outset, a process should be developed for establishing the criteria that the audit will use to support its conclusion and recommendations and to assess the integrity of the evidence and analysis. Management should be regularly informed of the progress of the audit, and the final report should contain no surprises.

Multidisciplinary

The broad scope of value-for-money auditing calls for audit personnel with a variety of skills and disciplines. For example, conducting a value-for-money audit or comprehensive audit may require an engineer to review capital acquisitions, an economist to audit information about the impact of regional or family island program, a statistician to design appropriate testing techniques, or a computer expert to audit value-for-money issues, associated with electronic data processing and so on.

Limits of the Concept

To avoid unrealistic expectations and unwarranted apprehensions, it is also important to understand the limitations of the value-for-money concepts. It is not the function of value-for-money auditing to pass judgment on the effectiveness of programs or to second-guess the decisions of an elected or governing body. On the contrary, value-for-money auditing determines whether the organization provides sufficient, accurate, relevant material to fulfill the responsibilities of those who make the decision.

Comprehensive auditing is not a panacea for an organization's every problem. It cannot identify every strength and weakness within an organization, though it should find the major ones. Management's function is to design, deliver, and control systems. In perspective, value-for-money auditing provides information to the extent that systems and controls are working well and identifies opportunities for improvements.

Elected Officials or Governing Bodies

Elected officials or governing bodies enjoy direct benefits from comprehensive auditing. They have the primary responsibility for determining the organization's goals, objectives, and key policies and for ensuring that the organization pursues these effectively and at reasonable cost economically and efficiently. As an independent assessment, the value-for-money auditing provides assurance that this is happening and, where appropriate, highlights specific management practices that can be improved. It provides an incentive to improve reporting and controls that should result in better systems for allocating resources, setting objectives, and rewarding performance.

Value-for-money audits help elected officials or governing bodies to discharge their responsibilities by identifying areas where they should work with management to improve administration, operations, and results. Value-for-money audits will undoubtedly increase "public confidence" in elected officials or members of governing bodies.

The Public

The ultimate beneficiary of value-for-money audits is you, the public, who provide the funds and benefit from public programs and services. Value-for-money auditing will now give the assurance about the organization's management, practices beyond that "conveyed" by audited financial statements and other various reports.

When value-for-money or performance audit reports are made available to the public, taxpayers obtain assurance that their elected or appointed representatives are kept informed as to whether the organization's "mandate" is being pursued in an economic, efficient, and effective manner. The public is given information to help judge whether resources are being managed with due regard to value for money.

Can effectiveness in government be measured? Well-established and widely used techniques are available for measuring economy and efficiency, so can effectiveness really be measured? It is recognized that by no means can all government programs be evaluated for effectiveness. Even in the case of programs that readily lend themselves to evaluation, it will not be perfect. Nevertheless, the professionals conducting value-for-money audits will find that information systems including financial systems will invariably produce most, if not all, of the information needed to assess the immediate outcome of a program. The evaluation of the effectiveness of programs should not be an esoteric mystery. If program evaluation is considered at the time when the program is being considered and designed, measures can be built in to collect data needed for evaluation.

Value-for-money auditing is here, and clearly, it is here to stay. It will take time therefore before the methodology is well established and widely known.

Complexities are plentiful in applying this widely ranging, multidisciplinary approach. It can only be executed efficiently with experienced staff. This new public sector approach to auditing is a direct response to increasing public concern over the need for improved management control and accountability in government.

Public-owned corporations need to be subjected to value-for-money auditing as they represent a sizeable portion of the total government, and they carry out all sorts of activities. It is necessary to determine clear boundaries of government agencies and corporations to enable the auditor general to fully execute mandates.

Governments are accountable to the parliament as they are required to answer questions about its policies and may alternately be repudiated by parliament. But, finally, government is accountable to the people through the mechanism of "elections."

Accountability and Mandate

Techniques have also changed and developed right up to the present date where we are mandated to carry out value-for-money audits.

To retain confidence, the Department of the Auditor General must continually improve and upgrade our services to justify the faith and sacred trust entrusted to them lest they lose credibility and their lawful right to be trustees of the people. Public accountability remains a fundamental primary responsibility of government and public sector organizations.

Effectiveness of Parliament: Public Accounts Committee

Parliamentary committees provide effective means of parliamentary scrutiny of the executive and its supporting bureaucracy. These committees serve to increase public accountability by undertaking their inquiries whenever possible in public and by reporting the results to parliament through their actions. Committees stimulate both parliamentary and public debate on government activities.

In practice, the public accounts committee concentrates most of its inquiries on matters included in audited reports of the auditor general, which are tabled in parliament. In principle, the committee does not concern itself with the merits of policy objectives and should conduct its business on nonparty political lines and take evidence primarily from the accounting officers of the audited department concerned. The committee submits reports to parliament on the results of its inquiries with recommendations for further actions.

The close cooperation between the auditor general and the public accounts committee within their respective independence is paramount to ensure effectiveness in their work.

CHAPTER 6

A New Focus

In the coming years, governments will continue struggling to balance the need to deliver a range of services with fewer and fewer resources while, at the same time, involving individuals, stakeholder groups, and communities in the tough choices that must be made. To meet the challenge, governments must be able to demonstrate clearly to their citizens that programs are producing the results they were designed to achieve, with the greatest efficiency. Governments must also know how well they are providing their services if they are to make sound decisions about those programs. This means that information about the actual results compared to the intended results of programs, and the cost of such programs, will be required.

Currently, government information systems are not focused on results. Measuring and reporting practices have traditionally focused on inputs (what resources have been acquired and used), process (what activities were undertaken and how), and compliance with spending authorities (was the money spent within the limits and for the purposes authorized). Less emphasis has been given to the outcomes achieved as a result of government efforts—that is, what the real impact has been on the lives of individuals and communities.

When government affects the lives of its citizens in as wide a range of social and economic activity as it does today, citizens have the right to know what their government intends to achieve and what it has actually accomplished. In other words, government must account to the public, through their elected representatives, for its intentions, its objectives and strategies, the costs of its strategies, and its actual results. Accountability for results can increase public confidence if citizens know that government programs are relevant and are effective and efficient in meeting the objectives that their government has set.

Providing Leadership

In responding to the economic, social, and political pressures facing them, some countries have chosen to re-focus their management efforts on results while others have dramatically changed the way they govern. In the USA, for example, the federal Government Performance and Results Act of 1993 (bill S20) provides for a series of pilot projects for performance measuring, performance budgeting, and performance reporting for its programs. During this period, Vice President Al Gore also undertook his national performance review. The final report, issued in September 1993, suggested that all agencies, whether they are pilots under bill S20 or not, develop performance measures and that performance objectives and results be made key elements in budget and management reviews.

Similar reforms have been undertaken at the state level in the USA. Oregon and Minnesota, along with the involvement of their citizens, defined a long-term vision for their future. Based on its twenty-year strategic plan, Oregon Shines, Oregon defined its interest in three key areas: (1) exceptional people, (2) an outstanding quality of life, and (3) a diverse, robust economy. Similarly, Minnesota Milestones defines the state's desired economic conditions, citizen behavior, and attitudes for the next thirty years. Both states believe that defining a shared vision for the long term, setting objectives, and measuring results will lead to a better future for their citizens.

The United Kingdom took a different approach to reform when it launched its Next Steps initiative in 1988. The aim of this initiative was to deliver government services more efficiently and effectively within available resources by transferring many of the executive functions of government to specially created executive agencies. These agencies were given greater freedom to operate within policy, resources, targets, and accountability guidelines set for them by the responsible minister. In effect, the relationship between the minister and an executive agency became one of "management by contract." As part of this "contract," agencies are expected to meet agreed targets for quality of service, financial performance, efficiency, and throughput.

Today, over half of the British civil service operates along the lines of the Next Steps initiative. The initiative generated renewed enthusiasm and increased commitment to improving value for money and quality of service.

In 1991, the United Kingdom government went on to introduce the citizen's charter as a way of raising the standards of public services and making them more responsive to users. The four main themes of the charter, which applies to all public services and privatized utilities, are to improve the quality of public services; provide choice, wherever possible, among competing providers; publish public service standards so that citizens can take action where the service is unacceptable; and ensure that public services give value for money within a tax bill the nation can afford.

Under the charter, public sector organizations may be subject to privatization, wider competition, or the contracting out of services. Local and national performance targets are published, as well as information on the standards achieved. The charter also provides for tougher, more independent inspectorates and better redress for citizens when things go wrong. By 1994, approximately thirty-eight individual charters had been published, covering such users as patients, passengers, council tenants, and jobseekers.

New Zealand, by contrast, has undergone a more radical change to bring about improvement in the performance of its public sector and its economy as a whole. A key aspect of its reform centered on changes to the accountability relationship between government and its administration. Ministers are now said to have a "purchase" interest in the goods and services produced by government departments, as well as an "ownership" interest in the public assets.

As part of the purchase interest, the chief executive of a government department is expected to produce certain outputs as agreed to with the responsible minister. The minister, in turn, is responsible for the choice of outputs (based on policy advice) as well as the outcomes that result from these outputs for the community. As the owner, government invests capital so that the departments can continue to produce the goods and services specified.

Chief executives are accountable to the minister for providing these goods and services within the agreed-upon price, quality, quantity, and timing. In turn, ministers are held accountable, through debate and questions in parliament, should they not make progress toward their declared intended outcomes. They may also be required to defend, before parliamentary select committees, their selection of purchased outputs and the links to outcomes.

These reforms are said to have helped government with its macromanagement of the economy. Ministers have a better understanding of what services departments will provide and how these services will affect the government's strategic goals. Consequently, they are able to make decisions with a clearer sense of the impact.

The achievement of results is central to the reforms undertaken by these countries, although the means for bringing this about has varied. The USA has taken a cautious approach, relaxing the rules and regulations governing program managers. The United Kingdom, in establishing executive agencies, has adopted private sector management techniques; it has also empowered its citizens by giving them the means to influence program choices and the delivery of services. New Zealand, by formally distinguishing between outputs and outcomes, has clarified responsibility and accountability for achieving outputs and outcomes. Legislators representing the spectrum of political parties have supported such reforms.

Changing the Management Culture

Underlying these public sector reforms was the need to encourage a culture of performance. By setting performance targets, measuring results, and linking consequences to performance, managers have gradually come to think in terms of outcomes rather than inputs and outputs. For example, as part of the Next Steps initiative in the United Kingdom, measurable goals for program performance are part of the employment contract for agency heads; in return for meeting these goals, the agency heads are given greater freedom in how their resources are spent. The citizen's charter, with its emphasis on performance standards in the public service, deliberately focuses management's attention on the interests of the customer. Poor performance, as defined by the consumer, has direct consequences to those who do not perform well. Patients, for example, may choose the services of another hospital, given information such as patient waiting lists. In the long run, public sector organizations that lose their market may also lose their funding.

In Australia and the United Kingdom, experience has shown that greater flexibility in managing seems to increase the likelihood that performance measures will be used. Based on this, the USA has relaxed central agency constraints in the areas of personnel, budget, and procurement for five of its agencies as part of a two-year project. The expectation is that managers will be more concerned with meeting performance targets than ensuring they comply with a set of strict rules and regulations.

Incentives from the private sector, such as performance-related pay and performance agreements, have also been used to focus management's efforts on the achievement of results. In the United Kingdom, the remuneration of the chief executive of an agency is linked to the achievement of key performance targets. In New Zealand, each chief executive signs a performance agreement, specifying the personal contribution expected of him or her.

Bringing about a focus on results can take time. The USA has recognized this and has taken a slow and cautious approach to implementing its Government Performance and Results Act. The act provides checkpoints so that Congress can review the results of the pilot projects before authorizing full implementation. As government has pointed out, the ultimate objective is to change agency and managerial behavior, not to create another bureaucratic system. Along with this change, the public must exercise some tolerance for errors as managers learn to adopt to a new way of managing. This tolerance may be difficult to gain, given the high standards of behavior and performance that the public has come to expect. Nonetheless, it is critical if the public sector is to increasingly manage and account for results.

Defining and Measuring Results

Citizens have a right to know what its government intends to achieve and what it actually does achieve for the range of government activities. To be accountable in this way, governments must clearly define, measure, and manage for the results they desire.

This is easier said than done. Governing in the public sector is extremely complex, involving a diverse range of programs. Governments need to balance the often-competing goals of effectiveness, efficiency, compliance, and probity with policy objectives that range from the delivery of goods and services to the setting of norms of conduct (such as fairness and equity). Unlike profit in the private sector, there is no simple, clear method for governments to define and measure their results.

Generally, governments find it easier to measure inputs and outputs since they control how resources are used and the level of activities that are undertaken. Increasingly, however, governments are describing their results in terms of outcomes. Many jurisdictions, where public sector management reform is under way, consider outcomes the ultimate expression of a government's intent. Outcomes, such as providing clean water, are of interest to legislators and the public alike, for they are a way of describing the real impact that a government has had on the lives of its citizens.

Defining and measuring outcomes, however, is seldom easy. It requires a clear understanding, at the outset, of the objectives or results expected from a program; although these objectives may be found in statutes, directives, strategic plans, or other documents of government, they may not be clearly understood. In fact, government programs may have multiple and conflicting objectives. Is a government's primary objective, for example, to operate programs in a way that promotes efficiency, or is it to provide equal access to services to as many citizens as possible? Even across government, the policy objectives of one public sector organization may, in some ways, contradict the objectives of another. Encouraging a healthy timber processing industry, for instance, may conflict with the objective of managing, protecting, and enhancing the environment.

Measuring outcomes is critical to knowing how well a government has met its objectives for improving the quality of life of its citizens. Developing outcome measures, though, can be difficult and contentious, in part because the link between program activities and program benefits is sometimes tenuous. Measuring an outcome may require time-consuming and costly processes, such as surveys, and could involve following program beneficiaries long after they have left the program. In light of this, less direct indicators, such as outputs, can serve as an intermediate measure of results. Nonetheless, it is on the basis of results—that is, the outcomes— that legislators and the public ultimately judge the success of government programs.

Output measures are a useful tool in the day-to-day management of programs and, in a results-based management system, would continue to be used. For example, by focusing on the cost, quantity, quality, and timeliness of outputs, program managers can begin to identify and balance competing priorities among program goals. Such measures also serve to focus program performance on the intended results. Measures such as quality, for instance, can force managers to think about their programs in terms of customer satisfaction, which, in turn, may lead to questions as to who consumes government programs. Understanding program clientele is a fundamental part of defining a program's objectives and its intended results.

Ultimately, it is important to know the outcomes of government programs that are a real interest to the public. Governments must find a way to clearly define the objectives they wish to achieve, measure their progress, and report to their citizens about how well they have achieved these objectives.

Managing for Results

Traditionally, parliamentary governments have been predominantly concerned with input controls and, to a lesser extent, with output measures. In effect, programs are largely controlled, administered, and reviewed on the basis of resource (financial, human, and capital) utilization. The main concern has been to ensure that (a) resources are applied only for purposes authorized, (b) amounts allocated are not exceeded, and (c) the program is managed according to internal rules and regulations for equity, probity, and prudence.

Issues such as economy and efficiency have become part of the management of government programs. Given this, some effort has been taken to measure the direct outputs of some programs. The average unit cost of processing a claim under an entitlement program is one such example. The implicit assumption of this management model is that the resources allocated to programs will produce the intended benefits for the specific target groups and, incidentally, for the wider public. Accountability for results is best served when programs and services are managed for results.

Many jurisdictions agree that the foundation for performance- or results-based management includes the following:

a) clearly stated, quantifiable, and realistic objectives that are linked to a government's strategic priorities
b) effective strategies to achieve those objectives
c) effective management structures and processes to ensure
  • the appropriate allocation of resources,
  • the commitment and motivation of program deliverers, and
  • administrative efficiency.

d) performance measuring and reporting, a cost-effective means for assessing performance (including inputs, outputs, and outcomes) and for reporting on whether the objectives have been achieved
e) real consequences for the success or failure of those involved in government activity

Within this framework for performance management are important issues that can complicate the achievement of results. For example, current practices in managing government programs, such as constraints on the use of personnel, materials, and resources, might actively discourage the achievement of results. A program manager who consistently underspends the budget allocation is more often rewarded with a budget reduction than with increased resources and responsibilities. In effect, managers often feel their performance is judged by how well they conform to rules and procedures rather than how well they achieve the intended outcomes or results of their programs.

A key part of understanding why results are as they are is to understand how the incentives work and how they can be modified for a system geared to results.

Accountability and Mandate

All public sector organizations should, by law, be required to have an annual declaration of intent, which states in advance what the organization intends to achieve during the year. The organization should monitor and measure its performance and at the end of the year report publicly on all those aspects. This allows the auditor general to have a much better base on which to work, but more importantly, it provides the assurance that is inherent in all aspects of the organization's activities.

Auditors have an awesome and important role to play in the development of their country. Government must provide and upgrade resources to continually improve public facilities and create economic opportunities that provide a quality life for all citizens.

The time has certainly come when national audit offices must function at their maximum level to provide its government and taxpayers with timely and useful information for decision making. Staff in the national audit offices must take on a new dynamic posture to cause the national audit office to be relevant in today's global society.

Presently, one-third of mankind lives in an environment of relative abundance, but two-thirds of mankind remains entrapped in a cruel web of circumstances that severely limit their rights to the basic necessities of life. They have not yet been able to achieve the transition of self-sustaining economic growth. They are caught in the grip of hunger and malnutrition, illiteracy, inadequate education, shrinking of opportunities, and corrosive poverty.

Public accountability is therefore a fundamental responsibility of governments, and public sector auditors must function as they are constitutionally mandated. If not, they will lose credibility and their lawful right to be trustees of the people.

Finally, I urge leaders, parliamentarians, public officials, and managers of corporations to be accountable to your responsibility and to be aware of the four major obstacles of life:

1. The difficulty of a true perspective
2. The difficulty of overestimation
3. The difficulty of underestimation
4. The difficulty of procrastination or taking no action at all

CONCLUSION

All forms of government must exhibit the highest standards of leadership accountability with the understanding that effective leadership knows that when they put people first, their effectiveness and efficiency improve. Effective leadership enables them to get things done through people. They learn what motivates others, and they transfer their own feelings of excitement and enthusiasm to those who follow their leadership.

A comprehensive accountability framework has been provided that integrates the following elements of effective performance management to guide all levels of governing—organizational and program performance, financial performance, legal compliance, and fairness, equity and probity—setting objectives and measuring performance, reporting on results, and making a legislative commitment and performance management in the public sector. But without effective leadership that demonstrates character and integrity at all levels of government, this comprehensive accountability framework cannot effect change in the public sector.

Government must exercise true leadership when implementing a strategic management approach that integrates strategic planning, policy development, research, and evaluation on an ongoing basis. This approach requires that operational plans be linked to their strategic plan; and performance measures must be identified for use in monitoring the effectiveness of programs, projects, and activities.

The primary element of accountability as seen by a public sector manager may well be to the government of the day, but the final accountability must be to the citizens. The importance of this accountability to the real owners should never be forgotten.

BIBLIOGRAPHY

"Business Dictionary."

Covey, Stephen.

Lombardi, Vince.

Martin Luther King, Jr. "American Civil Rights Activist, Minister."

"Merriam-Webster's Dictionary, An Encyclopedia Britannica Company."

Munroe, Dr. Myles. "Founding Sr. Pastor, Bahamas Faith Ministries; founding chairman of Myles Munroe International, international bestselling author, motivational speaker, and govt. consultant."

—. "The Power Of Vision." *The Principles And Power Of Vision: Keys to Achieving Personal and Corporate Destiny.* New Kensington, PA: Whitaker House, 2003.

Webster's New World Dictionary.

"Wikipedia, the free encyclopedia."

Historical Problems Studies and Documents by Professor G. R. Elton. Litt.D.